Stories
illustrated by
Pet Gotohda
and
Seb Burnett

Heinemann

Before Reading

In this story

 Ziggy

 Pod

Tricky words

- film
- cinema
- whispered
- popcorn
- floor
- screen
- attack

Introduce these tricky words and help the reader when they come across them later!

Story starter

Ziggy and Pod are aliens. They have been sent to Earth to find out how humans live. This time their mission was to find out what humans do for fun. They saw a poster advertising a new film called *ALIENS!*

Aliens at the Cinema

Ziggy and Pod had dressed up
as humans.

"Our mission today is to find out
what humans do for fun," said Ziggy.

"OK, boss," said Pod.

Ziggy and Pod saw a film poster.

NOW SHOWING – ALIENS!

Fun for everyone!

"We will go to the cinema!" said Ziggy.
"Then we will find out what humans
do for fun."

"Is my human costume OK?" asked Pod. "I have got one head, one arm and one leg."

"You fool!" said Ziggy. "Humans have one head, *two* arms and *two* legs."

"Sorry, boss," said Pod.

Ziggy and Pod went into the cinema.
"We will sit at the back and see what
the humans do," whispered Ziggy.
"Good thinking, boss," said Pod.

The aliens saw humans buying popcorn.

"We must buy some popcorn," said Ziggy.

"What do we do with popcorn?" asked Pod.

Ziggy looked at the floor.

"We must drop it on the floor," said Ziggy.

Ziggy and Pod sat at the back.
"We must look at that big screen,"
whispered Ziggy.
The film was about aliens on
Planet Zebulon. Some humans
wanted to attack the aliens!

Pod got up and jumped up and down.
"**STOP!**" he called out. "Don't hurt
our friends!"
Everyone said, "Sh-sh-sh-shush!"

Pod sat down.

"Look!" said Ziggy. "The aliens are attacking the humans!"

Pod got up and jumped up and down.

"*GO, ALIENS!*" he called out.

Everyone said, "Sh-sh-sh-shush!"

Ziggy and Pod had to leave the cinema. They went back to their spaceship to write their mission report.

MISSION REPORT TO HOME PLANET

Visit to Cinema

Humans go to the cinema for fun.

They buy popcorn and drop it on the floor.

They watch films about aliens!

They don't like it if you call out.

It isn't much fun!

Text Detective

- What was the film about?
- Why did Pod call out in the cinema?
- Do you think Ziggy and Pod are good at being humans?

Word Detective

- **Phonic Assessment:** Adding 'ing' to verbs ending in 'e' Page 5: Which letter must be dropped from 'have' before adding 'ing'?
- Page 11: Which letter must be dropped from 'leave' before adding 'ing'?
- Page 11: Which letter must be dropped from 'write' before adding 'ing'?

Super Speller

Can you spell these words from memory?

don't   looked   good

HA! HA! HA!

Q Where do aliens keep their sandwiches?

A In a launch box.

In this story

 Schoolboy Mo who is also Mole Man

 The Big Slug, his arch enemy

 President Dolphin

Tricky words

- Caribbean islands
- special
- anywhere
- ordinary
- luxury
- breaking
- together
- piece

Introduce these tricky words and help the reader when they come across them later!

Story starter

Mo is no ordinary boy. He has a very special nose. When he smells trouble, something amazing happens – Mo turns into a super-hero called Mole Man! One day, the class was learning about the Caribbean islands when Mo smelled bad trouble. Could it be his arch enemy – the Big Slug?

Mole Man
in the
Caribbean

THE CARIBBEAN

Mo was sitting in class.

"Today, we are going to learn about the Caribbean islands," said his teacher.

Just then, Mo's nose started twitching.

Mo had a special nose. He could smell trouble anywhere and he smelled *bad* trouble now.

"Can I get my pen?" asked Mo, and he ran off.

Mo rushed to his secret spot – and he burst out of his school clothes.

Mo was not an ordinary boy any more.

Mo was now ... **Mole Man!**

"Sniff, sniff," went Mole Man.

"Time to go digging."

Mole Man dug under land and sea.

He dug faster than the speed of light.

"I bet the Big Slug is behind this trouble," said Mole Man.
Soon his nose was twitching really fast.
"Time to tunnel *up*," said Mole Man.
He burst up through the ground.
He was on a Caribbean island!

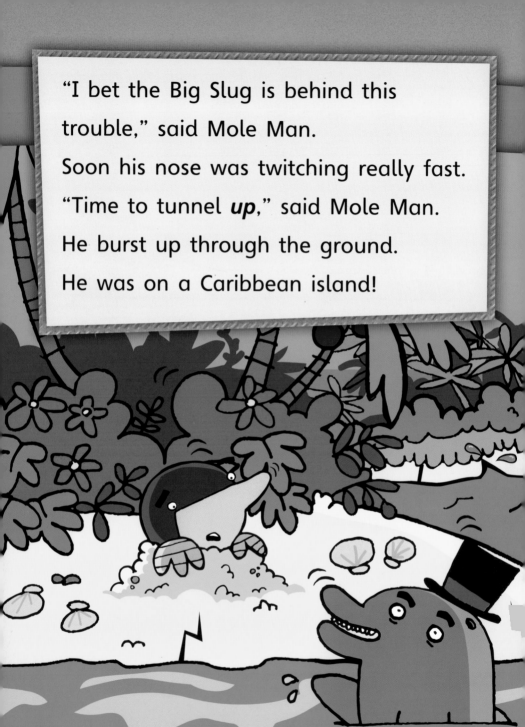

But something was wrong.

The island was in bits!

"Mole Man!" cried President Dolphin.

"The Big Slug's luxury ship is too big
and it's breaking up our island!"

"Tell your dolphins to come here,"
said Mole Man.

"**All** of them?" asked President Dolphin.

"All of them!" said Mole Man.

President Dolphin called his dolphins.

"I want you to push all the bits of
island back together," said Mole Man.

"1, 2, 3, **PUSH!**"

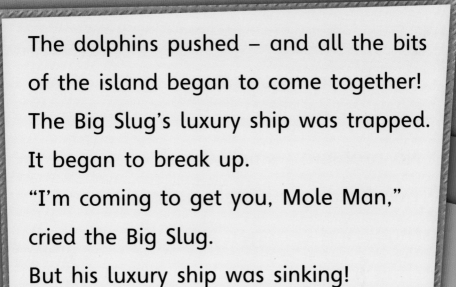

The dolphins pushed – and all the bits
of the island began to come together!
The Big Slug's luxury ship was trapped.
It began to break up.
"I'm coming to get you, Mole Man,"
cried the Big Slug.
But his luxury ship was sinking!

SLUG

The island was back in one piece again.
"Great work, Mole Man," said
President Dolphin.
"No problem," said Mole Man.
Then he dug all the way back to
school and changed into his
school clothes.

SEA SLUG

Mo rushed into class.

"Where on Earth have you been?"
said his teacher.

"Just to a Caribbean island," said Mo.

His teacher smiled.

"You and your little stories," he said.

Quiz

Text Detective

- Why was the island breaking up?
- Why was the Big Slug's ship sinking?
- If you were a super-hero, what special power would you have?

Word Detective

- **Phonic Assessment:** Doubling consonants
  Page 15: What must you add to 'sit' before adding 'ing'?
- Page 17: What must you add to 'dig' before adding 'ing'?
- Page 21: What must you add to 'swim' before adding 'ing'?

Super Speller

Can you spell these words from memory?

sitting   about   come

HA! HA! HA!

Q What did the dolphin say when another dolphin swam into him?

 You did that on porpoise!

24